Languages of the World

Italian

Sarah Medina

Heinemann Library
Chicago, Illinois

www.heinemannraintree.com
Visit our website to find out
more information about
Heinemann-Raintree books.

To order:

☎ Phone 888-454-2279

🖳 Visit www.heinemannraintree.com
to browse our catalog and order online.

Edited by Dan Nunn, Rebecca Rissman, and
    Catherine Veitch
Designed by Marcus Bell
Picture research by Ruth Blair
Production by Victoria Fitzgerald
Originated by Capstone Global Library Ltd
Printed and bound in China

15 14
10 9 8 7 6 5 4 3

**Library of Congress Cataloging-in-
Publication Data**
Medina, Sarah, 1960-
   Italian / Sarah Medina.
      p. cm.—(Languages of the world)
   Includes bibliographical references and index.
   ISBN 978-1-4329-5183-2—ISBN 978-1-4329-5185-
6 (pbk.) 1. Italian language—Textbooks for foreign
speakers—English. 2. Italian language—Grammar. 3.
Italian language—Spoken Italian. I. Title.
   PC1129.E5M43 2012
   458.2'421—dc22   2010043791

Acknowledgments

We would like to thank the following for permission to
reproduce photographs: Alamy pp. 5 (© dbimages), 21
(© Richard Broadwell), 22 (© Christine Webb), 25
(© Philip Scalia); Corbis pp. 7 (© Image Source), 23
(© GAETAN BALLY/Keystone), 24 (© Matthew Ashton/
AMA), 26 (© A. Green); Shutterstock pp. 6 (© Oliver-
Marc Steffen), 8 (© VolkOFF-ZS-BP), 9 (© blueking), 10
(© LeventeGyori), 11 (© Sarii Iuliia), 12 (© Andresr),
13 (© David Kelly), 14 (© Doreen Salcher), 15 (©
ShopArtGallery), 16 (© Tulchinskaya), 17 (© Bernad),
18 (© Brian K.), 19 (© Petr Jilek), 20 (© ARENA Creative),
27 (© Dima Fadeev), 28 (© Orange Line Media), 29
(© Tupungato).

Cover photograph of an adolescent girl reproduced with
permission of Getty Images (Marcy Maloy).

We would like to thank Nino Puma for his invaluable help
in the preparation of this book.

Every effort has been made to contact copyright holders
of material reproduced in this book. Any omissions will
be rectified in subsequent printings if notice is given to
the publisher.

All the Internet addresses (URLs) given in this book were
valid at the time of going to press. However, due to the
dynamic nature of the Internet, some addresses may have
changed, or sites may have changed or ceased to exist
since publication. While the author and publisher regret
any inconvenience this may cause readers, no responsibility
for any such changes can be accepted by either the author
or the publisher.

Contents

Italian words are in italics, *like this*. You can find out how to say them by looking in the pronunciation guide.

Italian Around the World

Italian is the main language of most people in Italy and San Marino. Some people in Malta, Switzerland, Vatican City, Croatia, Slovenia, Monaco, Albania, and Tunisia speak Italian, too.

San Marino

Italy

Many people in the United States speak Italian.

Italian is also spoken by some people in many other countries around the world—from France in Europe to the United States in North America, and Brazil in South America.

Who Speaks Italian?

Italian is the main language of about 60 million people. However, up to 90 million other people around the world can speak Italian, too. Italian is one of the world's top 20 most spoken languages.

In Tuscany, *cola* sounds like "hola"!

In different parts of Italy the way that people speak Italian varies a lot. The letter "c" is usually sounded, or pronounced, like a "k," but in Tuscany people pronounce it like an "h."

Italian and English

Some words, such as *pizza* and *piano*, are the same in Italian and English. Other words are very similar. Can you guess the meanings of the words below?

bicicletta   *studente*   *pinguino*   *famiglia*

(See page 32 for answers.)

English uses Italian words for different types of pasta, such as *spaghetti* and *macaroni*!

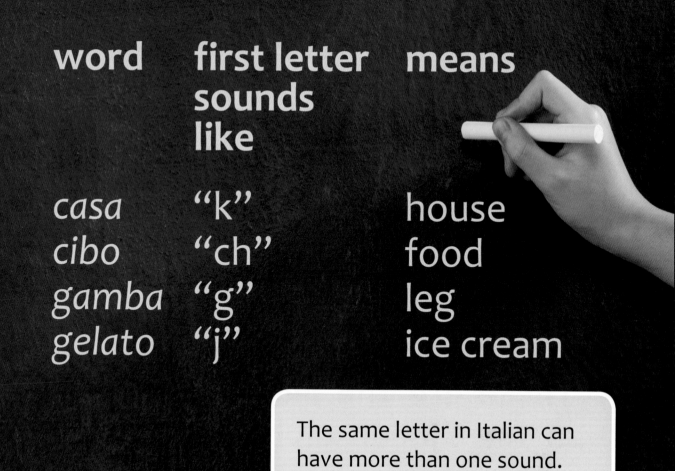

word	first letter sounds like	means
casa	"k"	house
cibo	"ch"	food
gamba	"g"	leg
gelato	"j"	ice cream

The same letter in Italian can have more than one sound.

Some letters in Italian have different sounds. The letter "c" can sound like a "k" or like "ch." The letter "g" can sound like a "g" in "good" or like a "j."

Learning Italian

Italian uses the same alphabet as English. However, unlike English, in Italian the letters j, k, w, x, and y are not used very often. They are mainly used in words that come from other languages.

These are the main letters in the Italian alphabet
abcdefghilmnopqrstuvz

These letters are not used very often
jkwxy

The word *pésca* means "fishing" in Italian, but *pèsca* means "peach!"

The Italian language uses special marks called accents to make vowels have different sounds. An acute accent looks like this: ´. A grave accent looks like this: `.

11

Saying Hello and Goodbye

Family and friends usually give each other a kiss on each cheek when they greet each other. People who do not know each other normally shake hands.

How to say it
handshake = *stretta di mano*
kiss = *bacio*

In Italian people often say "*buongiorno*" to say "hello" and "*addio*" to say "goodbye." "*Ciao*" can mean either "hello" or "goodbye."

Talking About Yourself

When people meet others for the first time they usually give their name. They may say "*Mi chiamo Sarah.*" "*Piacere*" means "Pleased to meet you."

How to say it
My name is ...
= *Mi chiamo* ...
Pleased to meet you
= *Piacere*

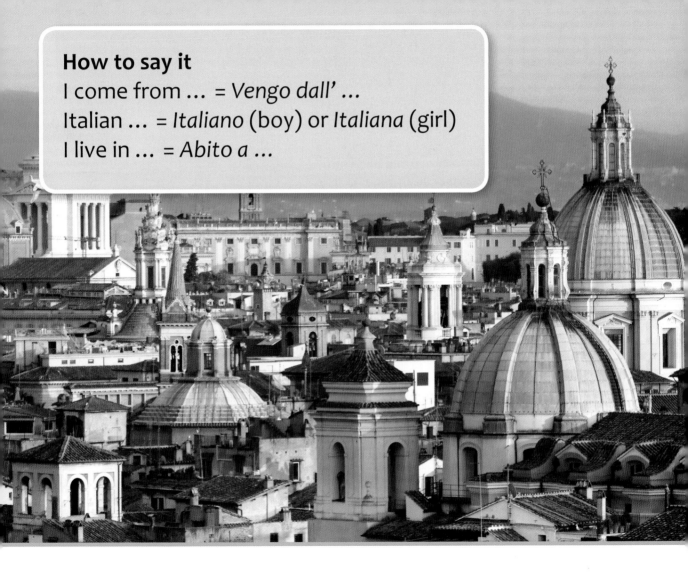

How to say it
I come from ... = *Vengo dall'* ...
Italian ... = *Italiano* (boy) or *Italiana* (girl)
I live in ... = *Abito a* ...

People often say where they are from.
For example, "*Vengo dall' Italia*" means
"I come from Italy." They may say where
they live. For example, "*Abito a Roma*"
("I live in Rome").

Asking About Others

It is polite to ask other people about themselves. The first thing people usually ask is someone's name. They say, "*Come ti chiami?*"

How to say it
What's your name? = *Come ti chiami?*

How to say it
Where are you from? = *Di dove sei?*
Where do you live? = *Dove abiti?*

To ask someone where they are from, people usually say *"Di dove sei?"* If they want to know where someone lives, they say *"Dove abiti?"*

At Home

In Italian cities most people live in apartments instead of houses. Some apartment buildings are new, but many are very old.

How to say it
apartment = *appartamento*
house = *casa*

In the countryside some families live in farmhouses. Some farmhouses are very large, with lots of rooms. Some even have swimming pools!

Family Life

In Italy, family is very important. In the south of the country, parents, children, and grandparents often live together.

How to say it
mother = *madre*
father = *padre*
brother = *fratello*
sister = *sorella*

How to say it
family = *famiglia*
grandfather = *nonno*
grandmother = *nonna*

A popular activity in Italy is the *passeggiata*, when people take an evening stroll. Many families enjoy talking to each other, as well as meeting other people, during the *passeggiata*.

At School

Many Italian children go to school at 8:30 a.m. At 1:30 p.m., they go home for lunch. However, they have to go to school from Monday to Saturday!

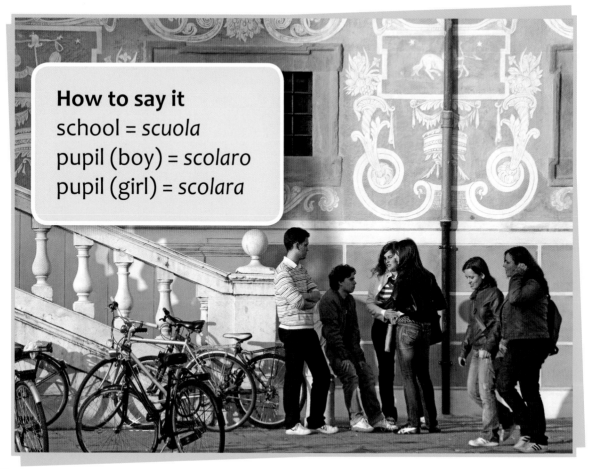

How to say it
school = *scuola*
pupil (boy) = *scolaro*
pupil (girl) = *scolara*

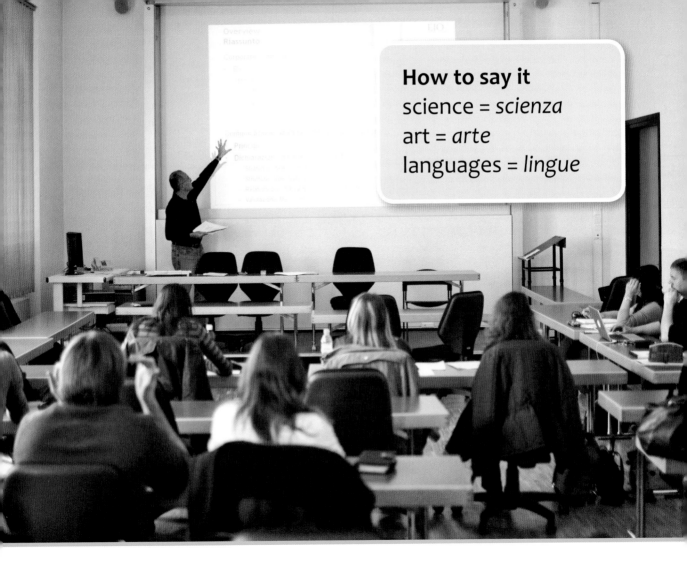

How to say it
science = *scienza*
art = *arte*
languages = *lingue*

Italian pupils can choose what type
of high school they go to. Schools
specialize in different subjects, such
as science, art, or languages.

Sports

Soccer is the main sport in Italy. All the big cities have their own soccer teams and stadiums—and thousands of fans!

How to say it
sports = *sport*
soccer = *calcio*
team = *squadra*
stadium = *stadio*

How to say it
ball = *palla*
lawn bowling = *bocce*

Many people in Italy enjoy the game of *bocce*, which is a type of lawn bowling. Two people, or two small teams, play against each other on special outdoor courts.

Food

In Italy, the main meal of the day is lunch. People often eat three courses: pasta, then meat with salad or vegetables, followed by fruit or dessert.

How to say it
lunch = *pranzo*
pasta = *pasta*
meat = *carne*
salad = *insalata*
vegetables = *verdure*
fruit = *frutta*
dessert = *dolce*

Many Italian foods are enjoyed around the world. People use Italian Parmesan cheese on pasta dishes. Some people enjoy Italian olives and olive oil. Pizza is popular everywhere!

Clothes

Many people in Italian-speaking countries relax in casual clothes like T-shirts and jeans. For work, people wear more formal clothes like suits, shirts, and skirts.

How to say it
T-shirt = *maglietta*
jeans = *jeans*
shirt = *camicia*
skirt = *gonna*

How to say it
fashion = *moda*
designer = *stilista*
suit = *vestito*
dress = *abito*

Most Italians love clothes. They are known for their good style. Some Italian fashion designers, such as Armani and Prada, are famous all over the world.

Pronunciation Guide

English	Italian	Pronunciation
apartment	*appartamento*	*a-par-ta-men-toh*
art	*arte*	*ahr-tay*
ball	*palla*	*pah-lah*
bathroom	*bagno*	*bah-nyo*
brother	*fratello*	*frah-tay-loh*
designer	*stilista*	*stee-lee-stah*
dessert	*dolce*	*dol-chay*
family	*famiglia*	*fah-mee-lee-yah*
farmhouse	*fattoria*	*fa-tour-ee-a*
fashion	*moda*	*moh-dah*
father	*padre*	*pah-dray*
fruit	*frutta*	*froo-tah*
goodbye	*addio*	*a-deo*
grandfather	*nonno*	*noh-noh*
grandmother	*nonna*	*noh-nah*
hello	*ciao*	*chow*
house	*casa*	*cah-zah*
I come from ...	*Vengo dall' ...*	*Ven-go da*
I live in ...	*Abito a ...*	*Ah-bee-toh ah*
Italian (boy)	*Italiano*	*Ee-tah-lee-ah-noh*
Italian (girl)	*Italiana*	*Ee-tah-lee-ah-nah*
Italy	*Italia*	*Ee-tah-lee-ah*
jeans	*jeans*	*jeens*
lawn bowling	*bocce*	*bo-chay*
kitchen	*cucina*	*koo-chee-nah*
languages	*lingue*	*lin-goo*

living room	soggiorno	soh-jor-noh
lunch	pranzo	prahn-tsoh
meat	carne	car-nay
mother	madre	mah-dray
My name is …	Mi chiamo …	Mee kee-ah-moh
olive oil	olio d'oliva	o-leo doh-lee-vah
olives	olive	oh-lee-veh
Parmesan cheese	Parmigiano	Par-mee-jah-noh
pasta	pasta	pah-stah
pizza	pizza	pee-tsah
Pleased to meet you	Piacere	Pee-ah-chay-ree
pupil (boy)	scolaro	s-co-la-row
pupil (girl)	scolara	s-co-la-ra
Rome	Roma	Roh-mah
salad	insalata	in-sah-lah-tah
school	scuola	skoo-oh-lah
science	scienza	shee-en-sah
shirt	camicia	cah-mee-tchah
sister	sorella	soh-ray-lah
skirt	gonna	goh-nah
soccer	calcio	cahl-choh
sports	sport	spohrt
stadium	stadio	stah-dee-oh
suit	vestito	vay-stee-toh
swimming pool	piscina	pee-shee-nah
team	squadra	skwah-drah
T-shirt	maglietta	mah-lee-ay-tah
vegetables	verdure	vayr-doo-ray
What's your name?	Come ti chiami?	Coh-may tee kee-ah-me?
Where are you from?	Di dove sei?	Dee doh-vay say?
Where do you live?	Dove abiti?	Doh-vay ah-bee-tee?

Find Out More

Books

Grodin, Elissa, and Cuomo, Mario. *C is for Ciao: An Italy Alphabet.*
   Ann Arbor: Sleeping Bear Press, 2008.
Parker, Vic. *We're From Italy.* Chicago: Heinemann Library, 2006.

Websites

kids.nationalgeographic.com/kids/places/find/italy/
www.pocanticohills.org/italy/italy.htm

Index

Meanings of the words on page 8

bicicletta = bicycle   *pinguino* = penguin
studente = student   *famiglia* = family